The Superwoman Lifestyle Blueprint

The Ultimate Woman's Guide to Embracing Her
Strengths, Defining Her All, and Living the Life She Was
Born to Live in Business, Beauty & Balance

Vicki Irvin

Copyright ©2011 Vicki Irvin All rights reserved.

This publication is licensed to the individual reader only. Duplication or distribution by any means, including email, disk, photocopy and recording, to a person other than the original purchaser is a violation of international copyright law.

Publisher: Vicki Irvin Enterprises,
6333 Old Branch Avenue, Suite 303, Temple Hills MD 20748

While they have made every effort to verify the information provided in this publication, neither the author nor the publisher assumes any responsibility for errors in, omissions from or different interpretation of the subject matter.

The information herein may be subject to varying laws and practices in different areas, states and countries. The reader assumes all responsibility for use of the information.

ISBN: 978-0615493602

This book is dedicated to all of the superwomen of the world who ever had a dream, hope or desire to be extraordinary.

It is also dedicated to my mother who had bigger plans for my life when I didn't have a plan of my own.

ABOUT VICKI IRVIN

Vicki Irvin is an entrepreneurial and business coach for women looking to go to the next level in life.

She has worked with thousands of people on how to build a better business and recognize the life they were born to live.

Her Superwoman Lifestyle community has thousands of followers across the country and her work has been included or featured by several media outlets including:

> *Essence Magazine, USA Today, Bloomberg Radio, Lifetime TV, CNN's HLN, Millionaire Blueprint Magazine and the Investor's Business Daily.*

Having worked in corporate America as a Human Resources professional and been witness to hundreds of people losing their jobs, Vicki stepped away from her traditional 9-5 job in pursuit of a more stable way to secure her financial future.

After discovering the blueprint to winning in business, she went on a mission to teach others how to turn their passions to profit and take back control of their future.

Visit us at www.SuperWomanLifestyle.com to join thousands of progressive women like yourself and become part of this phenomenal movement that is transforming lives one day at a time.

WHAT PEOPLE ARE SAYING ABOUT VICKI

If you have lots of ideas for business and you don't know where to start, do not let anything or anyone get in your way to learn how to create and monetize your brand with Vicki Irvin – who is sincere, successful and smart! With Vicki's help, I am focused, I have a brand and I have a system that is already opening doors to increasing my wealth and to helping others.

Willetta Love
Founder, Embrace With Love
www.EmbraceWithLove.com

Vicki helped me to create a brand within a market that is very crowded. She found a way to differentiate my business and make me stand out, while staying authentic to myself. I am so excited about the new direction of my business and now feel totally comfortable marketing myself!

Charisa Pruitt
The Seo Alliance Team
www.TheSeoAllianceTeam.com

I needed help with my business and decided to work with Vicki Irvin. The information I learned was amazing; she helped me put a new business model and strategy in place that resulted in instant profit just two weeks later! I can't wait to implement all of the other things I got from her!

Tracye McQuirter
Author, Coach
www.ByAnyGreensNecessary.com

Watching Vicki made me realize what was really possible. I came to her event with one idea, but then left and changed directions completely. I took her "riches in niches" and branding messages and put together an offline ad campaign based on some of the concepts from the materials and brought in a nice 5 figure income in month one! Thanks Vicki!

Karen Philippin-Kilpatrick
Attorney
www.SoFlowLaw.com

Vicki Irvin is more than a marketing coach – she is the premier Master Marketing Strategist. Vicki's wealth of knowledge and marketing experience is incredible. Vicki immediately pinpointed areas of improvement for my website and suggested tips to increase my clientele. I immediately implemented her recommendations. Nearly three weeks later, I am seeing amazing results. To top it off, her professionalism, exceptional communication style, and one-on-one sessions made the experience one to remember. Without doubt, Vicki Irvin is the best and unparalleled to others in the marketing arena.

Nisha Parker
Author, Coach
www.SynergyLounge.org

The branding session with Vicki was really an eye-opener for me and my business. She's the best when it comes to asking pointed questions which force you to search within yourself and become laser-focused. Her ideas are right on point. She provided me with an Ah-ha moment for my branding! I like her honesty, understanding and calm.

Stephanie Smith
The Etiquette Empress
www.EtiquetteEmpress.com

CONTENTS

	Page
Embracing the Superwoman Lifestyle	9
The Three Pillars of the Superwoman Lifestyle	17
• Business	19
• Beauty	29
• Balance	35
Your 5-Step Action Plan Blueprint for Living the Superwoman Lifestyle	41
1. Begin with Your Strengths	43
2. Build Yourself First	57
3. Become Extraordinary	67
4. Banish Fear	73
5. Believe in Every Opportunity	79
Begin the Change Today	83
Exercises	89
What People Are Saying About Vicki	95

Embracing the Superwoman Lifestyle

If you are not already living the life of your dreams – or at least moving towards that goal – then it's time to reinvent yourself and embrace the Superwoman within you.

Don't worry; I'm not going to tell you a bunch of stuff that is way over the top and untrue.

I am only going to tell you what is truly possible when you face some very real facts about yourself and your potential.

Being able to unleash your potential and attain a better level of balance and happiness in all the important facets of your life is a space most women want to move into.

A fulfilling life is on the horizon once you are able to experience the following:

- Financial independence
- Rewarding business or career
- Great relationships
- Happy and healthy family
- Time for your closest friends
- Me time

If that sounds far-fetched to you, don't worry, it's just that nobody has ever taught you how to live the Superwoman lifestyle.

But, believe me, it is more than attainable.

Why It's Not Just a Dream

Now I know you've probably heard people say that trying to be a Superwoman is the wrong way to live your life.

That it can end up leaving you disappointed and burned out and that it's just a pipe dream.

You've probably been told that the "Superwoman Syndrome" is a disease that will leave you beat down with nothing left to give.

Well I am here to challenge that myth.

I believe that not only can you live a Superwoman lifestyle, but that you should openly embrace it!

Let's face it; women are born nurturers and multi-taskers.

We have been taking care of our families since the beginning of time and running the household.

We are born with an inherited ability to juggle a wide range of responsibilities in our lives. So to try and give that up is virtually impossible.

I believe that the people who tell us we shouldn't make full use of these natural talents are leading us down the wrong road.

The Superwoman lifestyle is all about using your strengths and making them work in your favor

The Superwoman lifestyle is all about using your strengths and making them work in your favor.

That's exactly what you'll learn in this book.

Defining What's Important

As you continue reading this book, it's important to take inventory and think long and hard about what is important to you in your life.

Do not let anyone else define that for you. These should be your thoughts, your priorities and totally authentic to who you are.

In this book, I'll be sharing a number of exercises that will help you make positive changes in your life.

Having worked through these exercises with hundreds of other women, I know how valuable they can be in helping you shape your future.

By committing to these exercises, you are making time and space to carve out your own niche so that you can structure your life to achieve more for yourself.

You'll also be able to ensure that the things most important to you – like family, health and friends – are not sacrificed or neglected.

Being All You Can Be

Here is where most of us go wrong. As women, the number one mistake we make is comparing ourselves to other women and trying to emulate what we see and admire.

We look at what we see our friends and neighbors doing or perhaps even compare ourselves to our own mothers, trying to measure up.

And, while admiring someone else is perfectly fine, when you try to conduct yourself according to what someone else's life "looks" like, you put yourself through unnecessary stress and pain.

Yes, I happily admit that I am speaking from experience here.

I literally almost drove myself insane trying to mimic what I thought was perfection in other people.

It's not rocket science. Plain and simple, the reason it won't work for you is because you are not them.

The dynamic in our families, in our relationships and in all aspects of our lives is very different from that of other people.

If you are raising four children, why are you comparing yourself to the woman who has only one child that you think makes motherhood look easy, and breezes through each day so effortlessly?

Of course it's easier to move through the day with one kid versus four. It's like comparing apples to oranges.

If you have only been in business for one year, why are you so down on yourself for not yet attaining the same level of success as the woman who has been in business five years?

It's incongruent, it doesn't make sense and it puts unnecessary burdens on you to be someone you're not.

Avoiding Self-Sabotage

When you try to take on the life of someone else, you are not living a Superwoman lifestyle.

I almost drove myself insane trying to mimic what I thought was perfection in someone else

You are not being authentic. In fact, it's a form of self-sabotage.

But here is some good news!

Nine times out of ten, you already have what you need to live the Superwoman lifestyle.

You just need to identify it, unleash it, embrace it and then learn how to work it.

There are some key factors you need to get clear on as you embark on the quest to live your life on your own terms.

These factors include:

- Your own personal strengths and what makes you special

- The dreams and desires you want to achieve

- The people in your life that will help you achieve those

When you get clear about all these, you will know how to move towards your goals in every facet of your life on a consistent basis.

Feeling Good About Yourself

Ultimately, the place you want to be is going to bed at night feeling good about yourself…

- Sleeping easily knowing that you've taken care of the things that are important in your life – according to your own strengths and desires

- Knowing that you have moved at least 1% towards your goals that day

That's when you are able to have it all.

That's when you can be successful in each of the three pillars of the Superwoman lifestyle – Business, Beauty and Balance.

We'll talk more about those shortly.

You open yourself up to receive all you deserve when you:

- Give yourself permission to design your life on your own terms

- Stop worrying about and comparing yourself to other people

In order to get there, you first need to take some time to define your own terms and take the action steps towards living the Superwoman lifestyle.

In the rest of this book, I'm going to share more with you about the Superwoman lifestyle and show you how you can make it a reality in your life.

The Three Pillars of the Superwoman Lifestyle

First, we'll look in more detail at each of the three pillars that support the Superwoman lifestyle. These are:

- **Business**: A lot of women have great ideas and concepts they can turn into businesses but often they don't step forward with these ideas due to fear, self-doubt and the lack of knowledge on how to pull it all together

- **Beauty**: If you don't feel good about yourself on the inside and the outside, you will be limited in what you can achieve

- **Balance**: Too many women don't push forward with their own dreams because they give too much time to others and neglect themselves

Your Five Step Blueprint for Living the Superwoman Lifestyle

Next, we'll work through a five-step process designed to help you start living the Superwoman lifestyle right away.

As we go through these steps, you'll work through a series of questions and easy exercises to help you make the necessary changes in your life starting today.

These five steps are:

1) **Begin with your strengths:** Identify and embrace your strengths and your gifts to discover how you can profit from them

2) **Build yourself first:** Invest in your future by making a commitment to your personal growth

3) **Become extraordinary:** Stop believing the excuses that hold you back

4) **Banish fear:** Find your "Fearless Mode" to achieve your full potential

5) **Believe in every opportunity:** Start saying 'yes' today

Finally, we'll make sure that you are ready to get started and take action today so that you start seeing fast results.

I am proud to have you join me on this journey and wish you all the success you deserve.

The Three Pillars of the Superwoman Lifestyle

Superwoman Pillar 1: Business

Superwomen know how to translate their gifts and expertise into a business where they can help others, while creating financial security for themselves and their families.

Most women hesitate to do this for one of the following reasons:

• They don't know how to get started

• They don't have enough confidence to go out on their own

• They start but don't make the income they need to sustain themselves

Why We Need to Think Business

I spent many years in the corporate world as a Human Resources professional giving me a rare window into how a company operates and makes its most important decisions.

On a regular basis, it was a part of my job to deliver the devastating news of layoffs and cuts in retirement benefits to people who had been loyal employees of 20 and 30 years.

I began to see clearly that leaving your financial future – and that of your family – in the hands of another person, company or institution was a huge mistake.

People have been falsely led to believe that a job equals financial security.

Too many times, I have seen entire lives rocked and turned upside down.

Let me be clear about something. Job loyalty means nothing for one simple reason – it's not personal, it's business.

When a company needs to make a financial decision in order to stay in business, they do what they have to do in order to make that happen, even if it means your job.

They may like you very much and they may even be sad to see you go, but at the end of the day, they have a business to run and you will lose.

Leaving your financial future in the hands of another person or company is a huge mistake

Seeing this firsthand, I knew that I had to do something different before I was the next to go.

My First Venture

If you are one of the people who always knew what you were destined to do in life – and what you were talented at – then kudos to you.

I only wish I could have been so lucky!

In high school, I wasn't extremely motivated and had no desire to go to college.

If it wasn't for my mother literally filling out college applications for me, who knows where I would have ended up!

As I mentioned, my college education landed me in the field of Human Resources.

But, after recognizing I needed to do something else quickly, I decided it was time to become an entrepreneur.

I am living proof that entrepreneurs are not only born but also are people who decide to take matters into their own hands due to a wide range of life events and circumstances.

My first entrepreneurial endeavor was investing in real estate for myself.

Then, after experiencing some success with it, I decided to take it even further and teach other people how to do what I was doing.

I created a very successful coaching program helping people model my own personal success.

I grew the company to over $1 million in just 12 months – while juggling my marriage, raising my young son and tending to the other responsibilities that come with the game of life.

Now believe me when I say this didn't happen overnight or come easily.

Many women in business are struggling to maintain themselves and realize their full potential

I had a tidal wave of struggles and challenges to overcome, but I will tell you about all of that drama later.

My coaching program began receiving national attention and I soon found that other women were curious about how I was able to build and manage a successful business while still having time to tend to my family and myself.

That's when I realized how many other women in business were struggling to get their business to the level where they could sustain themselves and realize their full potential – without giving up or neglecting the things that mattered most to them in life.

And that's when I began thinking about how I could build a movement of women entrepreneurs prospering in business, beauty and balance.

Focus on Marketing

One of the most important lessons of my life was learning that, in order to operate a successful business, you must first focus on marketing yourself and your business.

Trusted mentors and other successful people warned me to grasp this concept first.

But, like most people, I thought I was smarter and could short-cut the process so I decided to do things my own way.

I figured that, as long as I focused on my skills and expertise, I would be a huge success.

Guess what? I fell flat on my face.

The truth of the matter is this…

No matter how great, gifted and talented we are at what we do, if we don't know how to attract, convert and retain clients and customers, we will never have a sustainable business.

The number one thing that matters in business is your ability to attract clients and customers so that they can actually find you.

You have to stop thinking of yourself as a 'coach' or an 'attorney' or whatever your expertise is.

You have to be a marketer first – regardless of your skill set, expertise or the core of your business.

There is a system and a method to client attraction, conversion and retention.

It wasn't until I had some failures that I was forced – out of desperation – to dive into marketing and learn these very concepts.

Once I started doing that, the real estate coaching program started to take off.

I had learned how to market the business and this stuff actually worked!

Investing in Yourself

There are two ways of succeeding in business – one is to blindly try out every option and keep falling flat on your face.

The other is to find people who are already successful and invest to learn from them.

The most important thing in business is your ability to attract clients and customers

As you can imagine, trying out every option and hitting roadblocks can cost you thousands and thousands of dollars – in both time and money.

If there is something you don't know how to do – or if you need a key piece of knowledge to get you to the next level – you have to find the people who are successful and who already know how to do it.

Then you invest in yourself by paying them and learning what they have to teach.

There is really no other way to succeed.

Every successful person – whether they are an entrepreneur, corporate executive or athlete – has a coach or mentor of some sort.

So, when my business wasn't reaching the levels I wanted, I invested in myself for several years to catch up and make up for all the time I lost doing it the wrong way.

I paid consultants, attended seminars, joined masterminds, took part in teleseminars, hired coaches...

You name it, I've done them all.

I did it all so that I could learn how to effectively market my business in any economy and continue to thrive. And that's when success came.

My success in business was because of what I learned from the coaches and mentors who showed me the way.

They had already made mistakes and figured out how to do it. So it was a no-brainer for me to invest with them to learn the right way.

My success in business was because of coaches and mentors who showed me the way

I would rather save money and time than go with trial and error and head in the wrong direction.

I have already traveled that road and it isn't pretty.

Self-investment is not a one-shot deal. When you are in business, it is a continuous process that never stops.

Every time you learn something new, the key is to take that one idea and implement it right away so that your business can explode and you quickly realize the return on your investment.

Why Women Hesitate

When I was first learning marketing and going to masterminds and conferences in the US, UK and around the world, I found the rooms filled with men. There were very few women.

That is when I decided to go on a mission to help other women entrepreneurs understand the concept of marketing.

I wanted them to be able to boost their businesses and take their lives to a whole new level.

Many women were raised in an environment where investing in yourself is not valued

If you have been working in your business for a long time trying to do it all alone and nothing is happening, then stop.

Without investing in learning what to do, and how to do it, nothing is ever going to change.

Until you learn how to invest in your most important asset, which is yourself, you will never realize your full potential – and you deserve more.

Keep the Customers Coming

Too many women in business are frustrated and on the verge of giving up.

The problem is they falsely believe that:

- Their ideas and concepts may not be so great after all, or

- They don't have what it takes to succeed.

Nothing could be further from the truth.

I feel that so many women have great products and services to give to the world that can positively affect the lives of others.

But they are often stalled at a point where attracting and acquiring customers is impossible – simply because they don't know how.

Building Autopilot Success Systems

Here is the reality. Being an entrepreneur is not just about how talented you are at what you do. It's about building systems that put your business on autopilot.

When you learn how to effectively market your business using proven systems and strategies, that's when you start to see the business turn around and you experience reinvention.

Once women in business grasp the concept of laying down systems, that is when they are able to build, grow and sustain viable operations and secure their financial futures.

The problem is that many women were not raised in an environment where investing in yourself is a value or concept that was ever taught or instilled.

Perhaps, like me, you were raised by parents from the generation where going to college and getting a "good" job with retirement benefits was the ultimate goal.

And most likely, you were raised in an environment where stepping out and pursuing your entrepreneurial dreams was reserved for foolish risk-takers with their heads in the clouds.

People who do this are often seen as out of touch with reality and headed down the wrong road. Sound familiar?

Choosing the Right Circles

Taking it a step further, you may be running in circles where if you tell people you are going to an educational seminar they will say it's a big waste of money and they will ridicule you.

Let's be crystal clear about something. They don't have a clue and that is not who you should be talking to.

Are you listening to people who know something about the entrepreneurial world and about marketing?

Or are you listening to people who work a 9-to-5?

Now I am not knocking anyone who works a 9-to-5. That was me too not that long ago and there is nothing wrong with it.

You have to pay attention to who you take advice from

My point is that you have to pay attention to who you take advice from.

What does a person in the traditional workforce know about the world of entrepreneurship? Having been on both sides, I know for a fact the mentality and mindsets of both are very different.

Ask yourself this, would you take advice from an attorney about heart surgery?

Of course not!

The smarter choice is to take advice from people who have become successful by investing in themselves.

Superwoman Pillar 2: Beauty

Beauty is an integral part of the Superwoman lifestyle but it's not only about how you look on the outside – it's also about the inside and how you feel at the end of the day.

We hear people say all of the time that "looks don't matter".

But what does matter is how you feel about how you look.

As a woman in business, you will often have to appear in front of people – whether it's meeting with one person, networking, presenting to a group or running your own live events.

If you do not feel good about how you look, you cannot give it 100%. That's not being shallow, that is being real.

You have to recognize your own strengths and gifts and create a sense of self

As women we have extra pep in our step when we feel well put together from head to toe.

When we are having a good hair day and wearing clothes we not only look good in, but feel confident in, we feel like we are winning.

On the flip side, the days we aren't happy with how we look, we are thrown off.

We are too preoccupied with our appearance to focus on the matters at hand.

The confidence level is way down and people can sense that. I know that you can relate to this.

Looking Good

It's hard not to be caught up in what society tells us is beauty. It's in our faces all the time, in magazines, on TV and everywhere.

But being a Superwoman is not about fitting in with the stereotype of being pretty.

There is always going to be someone prettier than you, so stop comparing yourself to other people, it's pointless.

You have to recognize your own strengths and gifts and create a sense of self.

It's not about physical beauty. It's more about how you feel and how you carry yourself.

Have you ever seen a woman walk into a room who society wouldn't necessarily call beautiful but she has 'something' that makes every head turn?

That is a women who has claimed her own beauty and created her own comfort zone, despite what society has said.

Beauty is about how you feel and how you carry yourself

That is what beauty is about for a Superwoman. See how we are once again defining our own terms here?

Feeling Good

Beauty is also about taking care of yourself through exercise, fitness and eating right.

If you're not exercising, you are not going to have the energy needed to push your business and your life to the levels where they were meant to be.

People winning in life go the extra mile and do what most other people don't do. In order to accomplish that, you need to have the stamina to do so.

Otherwise, you'll be burned out at the end of the day, feeling sluggish and ready to do nothing but go to sleep. Pure exhaustion will prevent you from accomplishing your goals.

But, when you have a regular exercise routine, it gives you energy. I know; I've done it both ways.

There was a period when I wasn't doing exercise and I was feeling sluggish – just wanting to close my eyes and sleep. But, when I exercise and engage in physical activity on a regular basis, I feel good about myself...

- The adrenaline is pumping

- I'm energized

- I'm recharged ready to give my all to every aspect of my life

On the other hand, we don't feel good if we are eating the wrong way and eating heavy food that's not digesting well.

When we do that, everything is slowing us down.

When you don't have a whole lot of energy for anything or anyone, that leads to guilt.

The last thing we want to do is slight our children or the people who are important to us simply because we aren't giving ourselves the proper fuel.

So I encourage women to do some form of exercise, whether it's walking, sprinting or going to the gym.

You should do whatever is going to give you the energy needed to succeed as well as take care of your health.

We have to give ourselves the best chance possible to stay disease-free and to stay healthy.

The fact we have family and children to take care of – and to be there for – should motivate us to make physical fitness a regular part of our lives.

So I challenge you to do just that.

Being Authentic

An important part of looking and feeling good is to stop looking at the next woman and stop trying to make yourself something you are not.

Some of the time, we women seem to feel we are kind of pitted against each other.

> *We have to give ourselves the best chance possible to stay disease-free and to stay healthy*

We may look at what others are doing and feel we are coming up short compared to them. If you ever find yourself in that situation, just stop. You can't be them, you can only be yourself.

There is nothing wrong with admiring someone and complimenting her. You may like the look of something she's wearing but it's probably not going to be a good look on you.

You can also learn from someone as a mentor or a coach and observe the characteristics and qualities that have made them successful.

But you can't be exactly like someone else. The only way to live your life authentically is to be yourself.

You need to let go of all that and focus on who you are so that you can be clear about what you want in your life.

It's much easier to have beauty when you're operating in authenticity.

When you are naturally yourself, people will sense it:

- They will hear it in what you say

- They will see it in how you look

- They will feel it from you and embrace it

You will have this natural aura of confidence because everything is so genuine.

If you ever tried for five minutes to be like someone else, you know it just doesn't work.

You have to be strong enough to know who you are and identify your strengths.

Trying to be like someone else goes against the Superwoman lifestyle.

The only way to live your life authentically is to be yourself

The Superwoman lifestyle is about embracing your own personal strengths and finding your all.

The Superwoman lifestyle is about living the life you were born to live on your terms. It's about embracing and loving yourself.

Superwoman Pillar 3: Balance

It's virtually impossible to achieve total balance in our lives, as this thing called life is unpredictable.

Something happens every other minute that throws us off what we thought was going to happen.

Defining a Space

While we can't achieve total balance, there is a way to define a space where you feel good about the time you give to the most important things in your life every day:

- Yourself
- Your children
- Your partner
- Your friends and family
- Your business

When you have defined that space – and you can go to bed without feeling guilty – that is when you have achieved a sense of balance within your life.

But if you find yourself going to bed at night tossing and turning because everything is out of whack and nothing has been accomplished, your life is out of alignment and there's no sense of balance there.

Start by realistically giving yourself a list of two or three things you want to accomplish each day.

If you are a person who can accomplish five things, then make it five.

But it must be attainable and within your reach.

If you set out with a list of 10 things you'll never accomplish – because it's unrealistic – you'll just disappoint yourself.

If doing two or three things in the day is moving you towards your goals, those two or three things are good enough.

Setting Your Own Standard

Living a Superwoman lifestyle is all about how you define it for yourself according to your own strengths, your own goals and your own threshold.

I no longer want you to focus on your best friend and what she is able to do and compare yourself to her. I only want you to focus on what is doable and satisfying to you.

Remember, this is about defining things for yourself according to the dynamics of your life – and your life only.

Balance is about what is right for you. It has nothing to do with others

Balance is about what's right for you. It has nothing to do with others.

I know because I can get caught up myself. I have a lot of girlfriends that I talk to and sometimes they tell me about all the activities they have their children enrolled in.

I have a good friend who has her daughter enrolled in about six different activities and my son is only enrolled in three.

So I'm thinking that maybe I'm not being such a great mom, and that I need to step it up!

Then I realize that our kids are very different.

- My child may have a bigger homework load than her child

- Her child may have a stronger capacity for focus than my child

- I may not be able to take my child to that many activities due to work

So why would I enroll my child in six things to keep up with my best friend if my child can't handle six different activities?

Not only is that pressure on me, it's also pressure on my son and that is totally unfair.

I'm not saying that these Superwoman principles are easy to apply in every situation.

After all, we are only human.

But, as with anything, practice and application makes it easier every time.

Applying the Strategy

Here's another example of a situation I applied that strategy to, just to show you how I am a work-in-progress myself. But it gets easier every time.

My son's teacher was sending out e-mails saying they were shutting down the school for a day to schedule conferences with parents, usually about 20 or 30 minutes each.

Practice makes it easier to apply these principles all the time

The teacher made it very clear they weren't mandatory conferences; they were optional.

At first I decided I didn't need a conference but then the chain emails started going back and forth showing how parents were scheduling their time slots and I started to panic.

It seemed like every parent was scheduling a conference for their child except me.

How was that going to look to everyone?

Like I didn't care about my son's progress?

Yup, I feared I was going to be judged!

But then I got a grip and thought about it. I asked myself what a woman living a Superwoman lifestyle would do and how she would handle this.

I had just recently had conversations with my son's teacher about his progress so I already knew how he was doing in school.

I asked myself what a woman living a Superwoman lifestyle would do

So I stopped myself and I remembered the lessons I teach to women all the time.

I knew I didn't need to have a conference.

There was nothing new she could tell me so why would I schedule a conference?

Just so that everybody on the e-mail list could see that I'm a 'good' mom too and I cared about my son?

So I took my own advice and sent an e-mail to the teacher saying "No thanks, I don't need a conference. I'm all set."

I almost got caught up in comparing myself to others but then I remembered my own teachings and pulled myself up by my Superwoman bootstraps!

It's the small things that are holding a lot of women back

At that moment, I felt so empowered!

It may sound like a small thing, but I know the small things are holding a lot of women back. It's something we all have to work on, but very doable.

I Can Sleep Easy

So you see; balance is about defining the space where, at the end of the day, you can rest your head and say:

- I took care of me
- I took care of my business
- My children and family are okay
- I feel good
- I'm going to sleep

That is balance within your life as you have defined it for yourself.

Your 5-Step Action Plan Blueprint for Living the Superwoman Lifestyle

Action Step 1: Begin With Your Strengths

Although the vast majority of women are not yet living the Superwoman lifestyle they want, it's easy to get started once you learn and follow the blueprint.

In fact, the truth is many are close to living it and they just don't know it.

Over the next few pages, I'll be sharing with you step-by-step how you can take action to start living the Superwoman lifestyle.

The first key is to begin with your strengths and identify how you can best profit from them. We'll cover this in three steps:

- Potential
- Passion
- Profiting

Potential

The first step is that you have to figure out how to unlock the potential that is lying dormant within you.

The fact is, we ALL have potential to do whatever we want to do.

There are no excuses.

I don't care how bad a hand you were dealt in life, whether you were born rich or poor or whether you grew up with or without supportive parents around. We all have the same potential.

In fact, many of the most successful people in all walks of life have faced challenges in their early lives.

What separates the successful people from the rest is what they decide to do with their potential.

Do you act on your potential? Or do you sit on it?

One of the worst things you can do is let yourself off the hook, by feeling sorry for yourself because of your circumstances, blaming other people or always saying how life has been so unfair to you.

When I work with people who have had it rough, I acknowledge that, I really do. I get it.

But I am more interested in having them take the lemons they were dealt and making lemonade with them.

You can take two equally gifted people growing up in the same difficult circumstances – whether due to sexual abuse, poverty, lacking a father figure or whatever, and

- One of them will draw strength from their experience and use it to push themselves forward so that they can help others, help themselves and create a better life for their own families

Do you act on your potential or do you sit on it?

- The other only focuses on the bad experience and never moves forward because they allow it to defeat them

So you see, one person acts on their potential and the other person sits on their potential and counts themselves out.

We all have stories of challenges we have faced in our lives. I certainly do. But I learned to acknowledge them and not to let them defeat me.

They do not define who I am as a person; they are just a part of my history. Instead, I look at what I am good at and focus on that.

Exercise 1: Acknowledge Your Past

So the first action I want you to take is to make a list of all the things that you consider not so great that have happened so far in your life. List all your big challenges.

Write them all out and put them on paper in front of you so that you have a visual of it. It's not just tucked away in your head.

Then just acknowledge them. Say to yourself:

"Yes this did happen to me but it doesn't have to define who I am for the rest of my life. Despite what has happened to me, I still have something of value to offer to the world that can help change other people's lives. I am still gifted despite it all."

What this does is gives you permission to move on, to pick up the pieces and unlock your true potential.

(Each of the exercises from the book is repeated at the back to give you a chance to work through them separately.)

Passion

Passion is defined as a "strong and barely controllable emotion".

It's a state or outburst of a certain emotion.

Working with women entrepreneurs, I find that most of the time they end up working on a business they have strong emotions about.

Perhaps you have lived a certain experience and recognize that other women in your shoes could benefit from what you have learned from that experience.

If you have solved the problem – or figured out the steps – now you may want to share it with other people because you feel so strongly about it.

When you work on a business that you are passionate about, you wake up each day energized and excited and overflowing with new ideas and concepts.

It's always easier to work on a business that excites you

You can't help yourself.

Many times you can barely sleep at night because this passion has you tossing and turning.

Exercise 2: Discover Your Passion

If you are just starting out in the idea phase of a business, the first thing I suggest you do is write down the things you are passionate about.

Write out the things that make you feel the way I just described.

Put them down on a list and then rank them in order of which one you are MOST passionate about.

If you are already an entrepreneur and you find yourself not loving it too much or even dreading it, it may be time to re-evaluate your situation again because you don't want to be burnt out.

It's always easier to work in a business that excites you as an entrepreneur – otherwise you won't give it your all.

Most people get into entrepreneurship to do something they love and create their own vision.

If you are not doing something you love, or even like, then you won't realize your full potential because you have no incentive to do so.

Recognize Your Gift

The next issue is whether, as well as being passionate about this thing, you are also gifted at it.

You need to know if you are good enough at it that your expertise can actually impact and change lives for other people.

Can you solve their problems with your gift or expertise?

So there are two parts to this.

You can have a passion about something, but – in order to profit from it – you also have to be good enough at it to help other people.

People will invest in programs, products and services that provide solutions for them.

Exercise 3: Discover Your Gift

So now I want you to list out the things you are gifted at. Think about how you are always helping other people with the same thing.

Maybe your advice is really good on how to deal with various life situations and you absolutely love being able to help them.

Maybe you are the person who all your friends and family call because you always have the perfect solution to their problems.

A lot of my clients get into Life Coaching and they have gone from spending hours on the phone helping people for FREE to creating the perfect life coaching business that they are now paid for.

THAT is profiting from your passions and not giving all your time and expertise away for free when you deserve to be compensated for it.

So whatever kind of coaching you are good at, that is a gift. If you are great at empowering other people to take action in life, that is a gift.

If you have been making jewelry for people as gifts for holidays and special occasions – and people rant and rave about how they love it – that is a gift; that is a talent.

So, instead of giving it away for free, you should make it into a business and profit from doing what you love.

In order to profit from your passion, you have to be good enough at it to help other people

Most companies start this way; someone is gifted at what they do and eventually they turn it into a full-fledged successful business that becomes nationally known.

So think long and hard about what you are really good at doing, write it down and identify with your gifts.

What may seem very easy and second nature to you is something that other people, who don't find it easy, would gladly pay YOU for. You should always remember that.

Women have a tendency to make light of their talents and never give themselves credit for them. If you are good, you are good. So embrace it.

Profiting

Now you have gone through the steps of:

- Acknowledging that you do have potential
- Unlocking that potential
- Identifying what you are gifted at
- Clarifying where your expertise and passions lie

The next step is to package it all up and make it into a business so that you can actually profit from it.

This is the really cool part.

The way to profit from your passion is to package everything up in a proven system.

While it's not possible to cover every aspect of profiting from your skills in this book, I want to touch on three of the most important elements.

Branding

Once you have nailed down your passion and unlocked your potential, the first step is coming up with the proper branding.

Branding is not about taglines and pretty logos. It is about creating a recognizable and relatable face for your business that makes money for you.

It has to be authentic to who you are and convey what you do for people who work with you – your clients.

Your prospective clients want to know what's in it for them and how you are going to solve their problem.

If your brand does not clearly communicate that, then you are turning people away and losing money.

So branding is a crucial part of the system I teach my clients for profiting from their gift.

If, after looking at your website or talking to you, people STILL don't understand what you offer and what you do, then that is a major problem.

It means there is a disconnect in your branding and in your messages. That has to be fixed immediately.

Building Your List

Secondly, if you do not have a way of establishing a list of prospects and building a relationship with them, you are not going to profit anywhere near as much as you should.

You cannot succeed as an entrepreneur until you build a growing list of qualified prospects.

You cannot succeed as an entrepreneur until you build a growing list of qualified prospects

This list is a group of people who are ready to jump on board with you voluntarily because they are interested in what you do.

They are people who have the potential to become your clients.

This is laser-focused marketing, rather than waking up each day wondering where your next client will come from and spending all your time on a wild-goose chase.

As I mentioned before, you have to become a marketer for your business first.

Your primary focus has to be on strategies for bringing in more clients and customers.

Nobody is going to invest in your products and services unless you capture their attention in some compelling way.

It's a relationship-building process very similar to dating; people need to get to know you.

You have to build trust with them because people won't waste time and money on products or services that don't offer value or with people who can't deliver what they promise.

We all know there are a whole bunch of people who don't deliver and consumers are leery of who they invest with.

So, your task is to make it easy for them to get to know you, like you and trust you and to prove that you can deliver something of value to them.

Your task is to make it as easy as possible for people to know, like and trust you

Packaging for Profit

When you have decided on your brand and started to build your list of qualified prospects, the key to making a profit is to package what you offer in a way that makes it attractive to prospects so they will want to buy from you.

It is critical that you do this in a way that sets you apart from everyone else doing what you do.

You need to offer something that literally makes you stand out from the crowd in a very bold way and catches the attention of your prospective customers.

I always urge my clients to think about what makes their service very different from others.

While there may be someone else in your industry offering the same services as you, I have found there is always something which each person does that is very different from the others.

Once we hone in on what their unique angle is, we go about incorporating that into the package so that it puts you in the spotlight and draws the extra attention you need to your business.

Packaging up your unique system is often the key to attracting more clients and customers than you can handle, which is the position we all want to be in.

Action Step 2: Build Yourself First

Too many women hold back their progress in life, in business and in everything else because of the natural urge to assist other people.

As women, we are natural nurturers and we like to take care of everyone else.

There is nothing wrong with helping others but you can help more people when you put yourself in the best position possible.

You do that by helping yourself first.

Using Your Gifts to Help Others

I find that so many women get into business for themselves because they have passions and gifts where they want to assist others through their work.

Unfortunately too many women in business end up giving away their skills, knowledge and expertise for much less than they are worth – and often times absolutely free.

One of the first things I do when working with women is show them the difference between running a business and working on a hobby.

One pays; the other doesn't. You decide.

If you want to help people on a large scale, the first thing you need to do is get yourself in the best position possible financially.

The more money you have, the more power you will have to reach the masses and effect change.

Philanthropists out there can give away money because they've worked hard and built themselves up first.

Now they can fulfill their mission of helping other people because they have the finances to do it.

You too should model this path if you truly want to help as many people as possible.

Preserving Your Wealth

Sometimes that instinct to nurture and help others extends to financial assistance.

If you are the person that everyone comes to for financial help – whether it's to meet their mortgage or pay the rent or pay a bill or get them out of some situation – you need to think about where it's going to put you financially.

If you want to help people, you need to get yourself in the best position possible financially

I have seen people lose everything because they have allowed themselves to be used:

- Constantly giving help to people who would not be there for them if the shoe were on the other foot

- Giving to people who manipulate them into thinking it's their duty to save the day

I have seen people in financial ruins because someone promised to pay them back.

Next thing they know, they can't pay their own mortgage because they will never see that money again.

You have to start recognizing things for what they are. Stand up for yourself and say 'no'.

It may be hard, but it is a part of reclaiming your own power, setting boundaries and living on your own terms.

It's a part of living The Superwoman lifestyle.

Choosing Your Circle

One of the lessons we can learn from the most successful people is that you are who you surround yourself with.

So today, I want to get you to look closely at your own inner circle – that means all of the people you are allowing in your space, whether they are friends, family, colleagues or acquaintances.

If you want to succeed, you need to surround yourself with other people who are positive, motivating and encouraging.

It's hard enough dealing with your own self-doubt but, when you couple that with the negativity of others, you are killing your dreams before you even get started.

The person who discourages you, ridicules you and tells you that you are just a dreamer is not someone you need to be in the company of.

Exercise 4: Choosing Your Circle

Draw up an inventory with two lists of some of the key people in your life.

Think about the effect people have on you after you leave their company.

On the first list, identify the people who uplift and motivate you.

On the second list, note the people who leave you feeling drained and deflated.

When you have drawn up these lists, you need to consciously choose to spend more time with the first group and very little time with the second group.

Some of the people on the second list, you should keep out of your life entirely – at least until they decide to change the way they think and behave.

This applies even if they are close friends and family.

This is how you start categorizing and changing your circle.

Thriving in Community

Women work best and thrive in community with other women on the same mission as them. That is a proven fact.

Do you know how powerful it is to be in a room full of positive women who understand and "get" you?

• Women working on their business and investing in themselves and their education

• Women who support you and want to see you succeed

That is one of the reasons investing in events and seminars is crucial to your success.

Events of this nature are life-changing and business-changing.

If you choose not to stay in community with others and choose not to attend events like that, you are hurting yourself.

When you attend these events, you not only get the tools you need to grow your business, you also get the encouragement and focus of like-minded people to boost you up.

It is virtually impossible to run a successful business alone.

Everyone needs help, guidance and mentorship.

This is why the most successful people in the world all have coaches and mentors showing them what to do and what not to do.

Someone like this lets you know when you are on the right track and will reel you in when you are going down the wrong path.

It cannot be done alone.

If you have been trying to do it alone and you feel frustrated and stuck, most likely you do not have the right environment on your side and you are not attached to the right people for guidance.

The most successful people in the world all have coaches and mentors showing them what to do

I get clients who come to me all the time and say they have been at their business for years trying to do it alone, and it just is not working.

Or they keep skipping from business to business and don't see any one thing all the way through. They are constantly in search of a better opportunity.

But the opportunity is not the problem; it's the lack of guidance.

Trust me, I have tried it.

I am guilty of trying this route myself. But I will never waste time like that again.

That is why I am always attending events and classes and teleclasses and getting involved with masterminds with my own coaches and mentors.

They ARE the secret weapons to my success. I wish I could take all the credit and say I'm just brilliant, but that is not the case.

Instead I stay plugged into other successful people and their events and teachings because that is how I learn to grow my own business.

The Winning Mindset

Obviously I have a family; I have a young son, a husband and more than one business to tend to. Yes, I am busy; we all are busy.

> *You can't expect to sell someone on working with you if you don't invest in yourself*

But continuing my education and belonging to mastermind groups is what keeps my business rolling.

I don't love hopping on a plane all the time from coast to coast, but it's mandatory if I want to keep growing my business, so I make it happen.

The minute I stop, things will go downhill.

That is the entrepreneurial mindset that makes you a winner compared to the person who convinces themselves they don't need to invest in themselves.

The entrepreneurial mindset is when someone sacrifices vacations for education.

I can't tell you how many clients come to me because they know I have coaches and mentors myself.

How can you be in business and not have your own mentors?

People will judge you on that, and you have to be authentic. You can't expect to sell someone on investing with you if they see that you do not even invest in yourself.

That's being a hypocrite and the savvy consumer will see right through you.

Being Prepared for the Feelings of Others

As you become more successful, you need to bear in mind that 'envy' and 'jealousy' are very close in meaning.

- Envy is a longing to possess something awarded to or achieved by another

- Jealousy is a feeling of resentment that another has gained something that you feel you more rightfully deserve

In my opinion, envy is a natural human emotion.

We see people with things and circumstances we are envious of; simply meaning we would love to have it for ourselves. Envy allows us to be happy for other people.

Jealousy however, has a negative undertone to it where the person is not happy for you and truly is bothered by your success.

The jealousy of others is part of the path to success

Admittedly, I am envious of lots of people and things, but I am still very happy for them. I'm sure you feel the same way.

I don't think anyone who says otherwise is telling the truth.

But let's talk about jealousy for a minute. Prepare for it, because it's coming.

Once you make the decision to go to the next level in life, it is almost inevitable that you will be met with the jealousy of close friends and family.

It is a part of being on a successful path that comes with the territory.

However, most people are ill-prepared for the backlash and wind up devastated when they are shunned by people they thought would be in their corner supporting them.

People will tell you that you "have changed" when the only thing that has changed about you is the decision to pursue something greater for yourself.

Sometimes success is a true indicator of who the people in your corner really are

Normally people feel this way because they are not happy in their own circumstances and it hurts them to see you moving on.

The best remedy for this is understanding. You need to understand that most people don't mean to be malicious; it's just an emotion they can't handle because of where they are in their life right now.

Yes, relationships and friendships have been irretrievably broken over jealousy. But, as long as you continue to be authentic to who you are, you can rest easy knowing you are guilty of nothing but self-improvement.

Sometimes success is a true indicator of who the people in your corner really are, so take it for what it is worth.

Action Step 3: Become Extraordinary

We all have to make a decision in life about where we want to be, how we want to be remembered and what we want to accomplish.

The easy option is blending in with the status quo. But that's really boring.

If you are even reading this book it's a pretty good indicator that you are looking to live an extraordinary life, so good for you!

I truly feel we all have the same potential in life.

Most of us have dreams and aspirations and the only thing that really holds most people back is the fear of the unknown and the fear of failure.

I've personally missed out on a lot of opportunities in my life based on fear and there came a point where I decided that I was not going to let fear win again.

I was not going to let fear win again because there is always something we end up regretting.

- If I had only said yes to this opportunity
- If I had just stepped out there on the stage and gone for it
- If I had only taken that risk

It is something you will go to your grave regretting.

What you have to do is be ready to trade in your ordinary life for an extraordinary one.

Most people don't do it, but a Superwoman will.

Less Crowded at the Top

You have to understand that it's less crowded at the top than it is at the bottom.

I say that because most people will never step out of their comfort zone and do something different.

Down at the bottom everyone blends in together, trying not to stand out too much and make any waves.

But making the decision to be extraordinary means doing things that your friends and family probably wouldn't do.

Most people never step outside their comfort zone

You need to start making moves and decisions that make people say:

"You're crazy"
"I wouldn't do that"
"That would never work"

That's when you know you're headed in the right direction.

That's when you get to experience things that are extraordinary in life. But you can't do that by following the status quo.

If you choose to stay in your comfort zone, you are going to have so many regrets.

Keeping the Fire Burning Inside

Most of us have a fire burning inside that is ready to explode. For some people, that fire will burn out after a while because they don't act on it.

But, for the people that step out there, for the risk-takers, for those who fight through the fear, they go on to lead extraordinary lives.

When you look back at what you did, you will realize:

- Everyone told you that you were crazy
- Everyone told you it wouldn't work
- Everyone told you to give up

Then you will feel good because you didn't listen to the nay-sayers and you followed your heart.

I know the problem is that many of us are bred into an ordinary lifestyle that sometimes we feel it's hard to break out of.

Sometimes we need to get out of our own way because we block a lot of opportunities

Sometimes working through some exercises and creating an inventory of what you want to do can help.

This again is a place a coach or mentor can really help you.

Getting In Our Own Way

One of the biggest things is that we sometimes need to get out of our own way because we block a lot of opportunities based on our own perception.

There is probably something extraordinary about us already that we don't recognize but others can clearly see.

Always remember that what is second nature to you is amazing to someone else.

It helps to have an outsider step in and show you these things and bring you through the process.

These revelations show you how stepping out of ordinary into extraordinary is very attainable and right at your fingertips.

Didn't I tell you that you were close to living a Superwoman lifestyle?

We need to stop listening to our self-doubts and stop the self-sabotage.

Instead, we need to listen to someone whom we trust, who is living a lifestyle that we aspire to live.

It's not easy to embrace every single portion of the Superwoman lifestyle alone and that's okay because we all need a coach and a mentor to help us through.

Stepping out of ordinary into extraordinary is very attainable

When I work with clients and help them figure out what's unique about them and their business, a whole new world is opened up for them.

Action Step 4: Banish Fear

Too many women miss out on opportunities because of fear but fear is a natural human emotion and you must learn how to work through it.

Whenever you talk to people, they often recall stories of a time that fear prevented them from accomplishing something.

So, let's get crystal clear about something. Fear is never going to go away.

You can either learn how to deal with it or you can allow it to cripple you. You have to make the decision.

I tell people that, in order to deal with fear, they must first find their "Fearless Mode".

In order to deal with fear, you must first find your "Fearless Mode"

I think everybody is able to reflect on challenging times in their life when they went through what seemed a devastating situation that they didn't even think they could pull through.

However they found out later that they were indeed able to survive it and push themselves forward.

For example, when you look to the future, you can probably see situations that make you uncomfortable.

Maybe it's something big on the horizon for you or an opportunity that's been presented to you that makes your heart beat through your chest.

The last thing you can do as a woman is allow fear to stop you from fulfilling the opportunity.

Everyone Feels Fear

I've talked to many successful speakers who've spoken in front of thousands of people and nobody could ever even tell they were scared.

But the truth is they were.

They tell me they are scared every time single time. It doesn't matter how many times they have done it.

It's just a natural human emotion.

It really helps me to realize that people I admire – great performers who seem to so easily step out on stage – are actually really nervous, just like me.

Once you realize that everybody has fear, you don't feel like such an anomaly and such an outsider.

It's comforting to know that everybody has to deal with and tackle this emotion.

What makes the difference is that some people allow it to cripple them while others just push through it, go on, and handle their business.

Facing Challenges

I suffered a huge challenge in my life when I lost my first baby. I thought I was having a healthy baby and then, after eight months of pregnancy, the doctors told me he wouldn't even make it to term.

When I realized that my unborn was going to die in my womb, this immense feeling of fear came over me that I can't even explain.

I was scared to be alone at night, I was scared of things I'd never been scared of before.

I thought having to deliver a stillborn baby was a situation I would never live through and be able to endure.

But I did survive it. I pushed through the fear and I rebounded.

Now, whenever I have challenges that come up in my life that scare me, I reflect back on that moment.

That is my own personal Fearless Mode that puts things in perspective for me.

If I could survive losing my first baby, I could survive anything else.

And while you may not have the same challenge as I have to reflect on, you definitely have one that you can relate to and draw strength from.

You have faced challenges that you will draw strength from

That is your Fearless Mode that will put things in perspective for you.

Before we move on to the next exercise, start to think about the big challenges that you have faced in your life.

Think about the big roadblocks you have come across that may have knocked you off your feet.

Remember situations where, for a time, you felt you couldn't see the light at the end of the tunnel.

Come up with as many of these challenges as you can.

You'll find that listing the most challenging situations you have already faced in your life helps put things in perspective for you.

It gives you a point of reference and a reminder of just how strong you are to have survived.

If you did it once, surely you can do it again!

While these situations may be in our past, we never usually allow ourselves to forget them because regret and guilt don't allow us to.

And, while the goal is not to forget them, we have to forgive ourselves for holding back.

Then we make the pledge to never allow this to happen again.

Taking these concepts out of your head and putting them on paper for a visual representation helps you to realize that you are resilient and capable of coming out on top.

Turning Challenges Into Opportunities

We have all allowed fear to stop us dead in our tracks before, but as with anything in life, we take these situations and turn them into opportunities moving forward.

So whenever fear creeps up again, I want you to look at your list and remember that you never want to feel that feeling of regret again.

Exercise 5: Finding Your Fearless Mode

To help you banish fear and stop it taking over your life, write down all of the things that have happened in your life that scared you so badly that you allowed them to stop you from pursing a great opportunity.

Once you have made your list of opportunities lost due to fear, acknowledge them and make the pledge to use them in a productive way.

These lost opportunities you have listed will now be life lessons for reflection and a reminder that you will never go back down that road again.

Action Step 5: Believe In Every Opportunity

I learned a long time ago from a mentor that I should say yes to every opportunity that comes my way.

As long as it's beneficial to your growth and it's ethical, you should get into the habit of having the word 'yes' automatically come out of your mouth when an opportunity presents itself.

Don't give yourself too much time to think about it and don't talk yourself out of doing something simply because you are scared.

It ties in with your Fearless Mode as when we're presented with opportunities that we know are awesome for us, the heart starts beating faster and our first instinct it to shy away from what is making us uncomfortable.

> ***Don't talk yourself out of doing something simply because you are scared***

When I'm hit with an opportunity to do a media appearance or appear before millions of people on TV, the first thing I say is yes, and then I work on the fear.

I have trained myself to do this and I have trained my clients to do the same. I don't give myself time to think about all these people watching me and I don't stop to think whether I should or shouldn't. I simply say yes.

When I am working with women entrepreneurs I teach them a secret I have been using for years to ensure they get stuff done fast.

Instead of working on a project and then announcing it, I tell them to announce it to the world first and then work on pulling it together.

The reason this is a habit you want to get into is because it forces you to rise to the occasion.

We women have a great deal of pride and we go out of our way to make sure we present a great image to the world.

So, as soon as we say yes and announce or confirm some type of opportunity, the deal is done and we have no choice but show up. We can't be let off the hook because we've made the commitment.

Employing this one simple strategy will help you get things done at lightning speed.

Trust me; try it.

Fear and Regret

If you turn down opportunities due to fear and allow it to win, it will be something you always regret.

You will always wonder what would've happened had you just said yes.

When opportunities come your way that could catapult your business or help you achieve a personal goal, you have to avoid coming up with excuses as to why you can't do it.

Fast action and fast implementation are both traits of successful business people and of the Superwoman

There's a great cliché that says 'when opportunity comes knocking, you had better be ready' and it's true.

There won't be too many times in life the same opportunity comes back. That moment will be long gone and it will be snatched up by somebody else.

How many people have thought of a great business idea but never acted upon it, never implemented it?

Truth is many people had the same idea but only one had the courage to say yes to the opportunity and go through with it.

Saying yes to opportunity is staying in the mode of taking fast action and fast implementation, both traits of successful business people and of the Superwoman.

Saying no to opportunities because you can't be in two places at once is a good place to be

People who embrace this philosophy are light-years ahead of the game.

The Time to Say No

As your business becomes more mature and successful, and you are truly living the Superwoman lifestyle, there will be a point where you can't say yes to everything simply because you will have so much on your plate.

Of course, you are going to have schedule conflicts and you are going to have to give up one thing for something else. But that's a great place to be in business, don't you agree?

You will have to say no to some opportunities due to time constraints and because it's impossible to be in two places at once.

But, even when you reach that stage, you will still be saying yes to the opportunities you can manage to take.

Someone in that situation is not saying no because of fear. She's saying no because she is now in a position where she has to pick and choose from all of the great opportunities coming her way

That means she has reached her stride.

Begin the Change Today

After you've gone through all of these steps, I want you to see that you are just a few steps away from living a Superwoman lifestyle.

Quite easily we have just defined your Superwoman Lifestyle Blueprint!

This blueprint is unique to you because it is defined by you on your terms, and fits within the dynamic of your life.

How empowering is that?

In five simple steps you have literally shaved years off of your learning curve on how to live a fulfilling life in Business, Beauty & Balance.

You have identified your strengths and the gifts that you have to offer to the world by realizing your potential, figuring out your true passions and learning how to turn those passions into profit.

You have learned an important lesson on how to put yourself first

Next, you learned an important lesson on how to put yourself first by building your business and setting yourself up for success.

You have learned that you can help more people in the world by first putting yourself in the best position possible to do so.

You have moved your circle to one of positive energy and you have learned not to allow other people to manipulate you. As a result, you have reclaimed your power!

Quite remarkably, you have learned how to become extraordinary instead of blending in with the crowd.

You have made the decision to step out of your own way and allow your light to shine.

You have recognized and acknowledged that fear is a natural human emotion that will never go away.

But you are now equipped to take fear on by finding your Fearless Mode and pushing through it.

Never again will you allow fear to stop you from being extraordinary and daring to be different.

Fear will never again win.

Lastly, you have learned to believe in opportunities and say yes to them as they come your way.

You now understand that opportunity is meant to be taken and each one represents a pathway to achieving your goals and living the life you were born to live.

You are now equipped to take fear on by finding your Fearless Mode

I bet you didn't even realize you have accomplished so much, just by reading this book, but congratulations, you are now light-years ahead of the game!

Living the Superwoman lifestyle is not about changing who you are.

You can't be someone that you are not. That's not what we're trying to do.

We are simply taking some strategic steps to unlock your potential and reinvent the framework you already have in place.

The Superwoman lifestyle is about defining our strengths and saying:

- I'm totally comfortable with this
- I am unique and I am special
- This is what I can do
- I am moving towards my goals each day
- I choose to be extraordinary

Trying to be someone else is disingenuous, it's inauthentic and it's not going to work long-term.

I want women living the Superwoman lifestyle to be comfortable with themselves at the end of the day.

Embrace your natural talents and use them to effect change while profiting from doing what you love

I want you take your natural born gifts and talents that you have, embrace them and use them to help effect change while profiting from doing what you love.

The Superwoman lifestyle isn't about living some perfect life.

It's not about hiding who we are or being ashamed of our past mistakes and struggles.

Embrace your past, you can't change it

It's more about using our experiences to better both ourselves and the lives of others.

That's what I help women to do.

Love yourself just the way you are, simply turn up the volume.

So what happens next?

Well the first key is always to take action.

In theory, it takes 21 days to make or break a habit.

So, when you start to follow these principles, you should start to see significant changes in your life fairly quickly.

Once you begin to employ the philosophies of the Superwoman lifestyle, people will say 'there's something different about you'.

- You are confident
- You have self-esteem
- You have a strong sense of self

Other people notice that.

Remember, for every woman you admire, there are 20 women looking at and admiring you.

Congratulations and let me be the first to welcome you to the Superwoman lifestyle!

Visit us at www.SuperWomanLifestyle.com to join thousands of progressive women like yourself and become part of this phenomenal movement that is transforming lives one day at a time.

Exercises

The exercises from the book are repeated on the following pages to give you the chance to work through them separately.

Exercise 1: Acknowledge Your Past

The first action I want you to take is to make a list of all the things which you consider not so great that have happened so far in your life. List all your big challenges.

Write them all out and put the paper in front of you so that you have a visual of it, it's not just tucked away in your head.

Then just acknowledge them. Say to yourself:

"Yes this did happen to me but it doesn't have to define who I am for the rest of my life. Despite what has happened to me, I still have something of value to offer to the world that can help change other people's lives. I am still gifted despite it all."

What this does is gives you permission to move on, to pick up the pieces and unlock your true potential.

Exercise 2: Discover Your Passion

If you are just starting out in the idea phase of a business, the first thing I suggest you do is write down the things you are passionate about.

Write out the things that make you feel the way I just described.

Put them down on a list and then rank them in order of which one you are MOST passionate about.

Exercise 3: Discover Your Gift

Now I want you to list out the things you are gifted at. Think about how you are always helping other people with the same thing.

Maybe your advice is really good on how to deal with various life situations and you absolutely love being able to help them.

Maybe you are the person who all your friends and family call because you always have the perfect solution to their problems.

Exercise 4: Choosing Your Circle

Draw up an inventory with two lists of some of the key people in your life.

Think about the effect people have on you after you leave their company.

On the first list, identify the people who uplift and motivate you.

On the second list, note the people who leave you feeling drained and deflated.

Exercise 5: Finding Your Fearless Mode

To help you banish fear and stop it taking over your life, write down all of the things that have happened in your life which scared you so badly that you allowed them to stop you from pursing a great opportunity.

Once you have made your list of opportunities lost due to fear, acknowledge them and make the pledge to use them in a productive way.

These lost opportunities you have listed will now be life lessons for reflection and a reminder that you will never go back down that road again.

What People Are Saying About Vicki

Vicki has pulled back the curtains and demystified the marketing process. She provided step by step guidance that helped me gain insight and clarify my purpose. My greatest learning curve was focusing on and crafting a clear & compelling message and communicating it effectively to potential clients. With Vicki's direction, I have been able to craft and communicate my message successfully and I now have a plan of action and the guidance I need to implement it immediately.

Latalya Palmer-Lewis
Unleash Your Genius Coach
www.CoachLatalya.com

I have increased my net worth by $300,000 since June 2008 using Vicki Irvin's principles and have made more than $100,000 in profit in just the first 12 months. Vicki only teaches win-win solutions for all parties and with the highest moral and ethical standards for her students. This is the only way to do business and it will give you the personal satisfaction that you are making a positive difference in the business community. Simply amazing!

Cynthia Gordan-Nicks
CGN Investment
www.NickBuysHouses.com

I attended a Vicki Irvin event which was a changing point in my life and my business. Her knowledge and encouragement were exactly what I needed in order to have a serious breakthrough before I gave up! As a result of her event, I now have an automated business, I'm building my list and every day is exciting. She has literally reinvented my business to one that is growing consistently.

Katina Davis
The Eco Green Queen
www.GreenForALiving.com

I have only recently joined Vicki Irvin's Marketing and Implementation coaching program and already I have a system in place to profit for my business. I have had my business for years and have been struggling to pull all my ideas together. Her marketing system for implementation has already resulted in two new clients valued at $15,000 for my event planning business! The best part is that I can repeat this process over and over again and keep profiting.

Bonita Parker
The Event Planning Queen
www.Elegant-Expose.com

I recently worked with Vicki on building my Brand and I am thrilled! I am currently on the TV show America Now and also in production for another TV show coming out soon. Most recently I got booked to appear on the TV show "The Doctors" to premiere my new fitness product "Fi-Danz" in front of millions of people. Vicki helped me develop an appealing Brand that conveys who I am in the fitness industry and as a result, mega media opportunities are coming my way! There is nobody better than Vicki!

Basheerah Amad
Celebrity Fitness Trainer
www.BasheerahAmad.com

Vicki's branding experience was the most productive step towards marketing my business expertise that I have taken so far. She developed a branded Five Step S.P.A.C.E. Transformation System that clearly conveys my value to prospective customers. It's brilliant! Thank you, Vicki!

Mary Roberts
Successful Spaces
www.SuccessfulStudentEnvironments.com

Vicki Irvin has been the "find" of the decade for me. With her coaching, mentoring and support, I have been able to complete my first book, speak on stage at live events, and I am now in the process of creating my affiliate marketing coaching program for women entrepreneurs! It's awesome when you can find the right person to hone your skills and talents so that you can enrich the lives of others with your gifts. Thanks Vicki.

Kimberly Davis,
Author, Speaker, Coach
www.KimADavis

Vicki Irvin is the BEST marketing and business coach/mentor that I have had the opportunity to work with. Her teaching methods are refreshing with new and innovative ways to be successful in any business that you may have. The tools that she has equipped me with through the coaching sessions have given me everything that I need to be successful in my business. If you have a business but don't know what to do or what works and what doesn't.... Vicki is the one to ask!

Doreena Walker
The Menopause Coaching Queen
www.TheMenopauseCoachingQueen.com

The inspiration, perspective – and time to think – from Vicki Irvin's event led me to make a major decision absolutely key to growing my business — hiring a communications and marketing expert. For too long, I was trying to do this important job on my own. It was only ONE of many revelations I had that I acted on from Vicki's event that has profoundly and positively affected my business.

Debbie Phillips
Women on Fire®
www.BeAWomanOnFire.com

Vicki is not only brilliant and talented; she's a pleasure to work with. She has an amazing ability to look at all the work and effort you have already done and find your brand within your own words. Her passion for setting her clients apart from the rest truly shows.

Cheryl Paulsen
Cheryl Paulsen Coaching
www.CherylPaulsenCoaching.com

I was blown away by the marketing strategies and techniques that I learned from Vicki. Even though I have an MBA, I learned brand new marketing strategies I had never heard before because you can't learn this from a textbook. You get real-life proven techniques from entrepreneurs who have done it and are still doing it! Not theory and academic marking ideas. Vicki introduces women to the proven marketing systems, strategies and concepts that successful entrepreneurs are using today to earn six figures and seven figures!

Adwoa M. Jones
Founder, Crystal Clear Interviews
www.PrepareforYourInterview.com

It has been a pleasure being one of Vicki Irvin's coaching clients. I've been gleaning from her since 2008. She is patient, she is thorough but most of all she is good at what she does. I love the fact that she gives individualized attention. The strategies I learned are the foundation of success for every hopeful entrepreneur. I'm glad to have made an investment in my education because the principles that Vicki is teaching will take my business to the next level & beyond!

Shelly King
Destine 4 Change, LLC
www.Destine4Change.com

Made in the USA
Charleston, SC
17 March 2013